AF700142

ROCKY MOUNTAINS

ROCKY MOUNTAINS

PHOTOGRAPHY • DAVID MUENCH

TEXT • DAVID SUMNER

Flinsch Peak and Old Woman Lake, Glacier National Park, Montana.

ROCKY MOUNTAINS

For those who watch over the Rocky Mountains today . . . who work for the continued preservation and well being of this great range.

"The earth was created by the assistance of the sun, and it should be left as it was," said Chief Joseph of the Nez Perce, "The country was made without lines of demarcation, and it is no man's business to divide it . . . The earth and myself are of one mind. The measure of our bodies are the same."

CONTENTS

International Standard Book Number 0-912856-16-5
Library of Congress Catalog Number 74-33864

Copyright© 1975 by Graphic Arts Center Publishing Co.

P.O. Box 10306 • Portland, Oregon 97210 • 503/224-7777
Publisher • Charles H. Belding
Designer • Bonnie Muench
Text • David Sumner
Printer • Graphic Arts Center
Bindery • Lincoln & Allen
Printed in the United States of America
Sixth Printing

September in Crystal River Canyon, Elk Mountains, Colorado.

Parry primrose, San Juan Range, Colorado. Right: Whitebark roots, Sawtooth Wilderness, Idaho. Pages 4-5: The Continental Divide bulks above the high plains, Augusta, Montana.

Notes of a flute, the roar of a cascade, Needle Mountains, San Juan Range, Colorado. Left: Falls on Henson Creek near Lake City. Pages 8-9: January morning, Mt. Wilson and Wilson Peak in the lofty San Miguel Range near Telluride.

Summer storm passes over Jupiter Peak (13,830 feet), Needle Mountains, Colorado. Left: Tilted volcanics and Vermillion Peak (13,894 feet) high above Trout Lake in San Juan Range.

Rolling expanse of alpine tundra above Cinnamon Pass in heart of the San Juan Range's historic gold and silver country. Right: Needle Creek and boulders, Chicago Basin along the western margin of Colorado's Weminuche Wilderness.

Joy of reaching the 14,309 foot summit of Uncompahgre Peak.
Left: Crest of the Needles, Sunlight Peak (14,059 feet) and Windom Peak (14,087 feet) center, from the summit of Jupiter Peak, Colorado.

Dolly Varden Mountain presides over American Flats and
mining relic in Engineer Pass, Colorado. Right: Precambrian walls
of Uncompahgre River Gorge above Ouray in the San Juans.

Marmot resident on Uncompahgre Peak overlooking the upper Cimarron River Basin with shrouded Wetterhorn Peak (14,017 feet) and Coxcomb Peak (13,656 feet) to the west. Left: The spring flow of Sneffels Creek and Parry primrose in Yankee Boy Basin, Colorado. Pages 20-21: Autumn transformation below north face of Mount Sneffels (14,150 feet), San Juan Range.

Aspen trunks veil Wilson Peak (14,017 feet) in San Miguel Range. Left: Aspen color along Canyon Creek above Ouray. Pages 24-25: May storm reveals peaks of the Grenadier Range, Animas River Canyon.

Mount Abram's summit dome, site of many a winter avalanche, marks the southern rim of a deep mountain amphitheatre surrounding the historic mining town of Ouray, San Juan Range. Right: October flurries powder the San Miguel Range above Telluride, Colorado.

October morning walk with the dogs, San Miguel Range in backdrop, Colorado. Left: United States Mountain rising (13,036 feet) towers over road to Camp Bird and Sneffels, San Juan Range.

PROLOGUE: THE RIDGE

Near the upthrust, partially demolished midpoint of central Colorado's Sangre de Cristo Range, a nameless 13,150-foot ridge traces a long fishhook of an arc round the head of a steeply glaciated cirque. Like many others in the Rocky Mountains, it is neither spectacular nor unique. Eastward it runs straight and narrow—a thin, ragged rim of smashed up rock—but to the west it bends sharply and spreads to a broad slanting, grassy bench. Its entire length is barely a mile. And at either end it abruptly dies, engulfed by the flanks of dark peaks which bulk more than 1,000 feet above it.

On this ridge, which tops out high above timberline, dwarf alpine plants—grasses, sedges, herbs, small wildflowers and two-inch shrubs—survive as best they can. Angular, frost-fractured chunks of rock, most no larger than a clenched fist, lie strewn about the bench as if they'd been hurled in an inconclusive Stone Age battle. Splotches of crusty green lichen cling to many of these fragments, and in their protected lees, occasional mosses have taken precarious root.

Most animals avoid these heights; instinct told them long ago that the ridge offers little of benefit and much to endanger. Come summer, flies and solitary bumblebees will drift upward to the bright alpine blooms on the bench, and it's possible that a pair of rosy finches, or water pipits, or ptarmigan might nest by the broken, sheltering rocks—or that bighorn sheep might graze the forage—or that a coyote, since his inquisitive kin have nosed into just about every other corner of the West, might periodically wander by. None, however, would willfully venture onto the straight end of the fishhook; barren rock does not attract life.

Climate at 13,150 feet ranges from pleasant to harsh to brutal, but mostly it is severe. In winter, hurricane force winds often slam across the ridge and snow is possible any day of the year. Temperatures stay low; on a hot August day, the mercury may inch upward to 60° F.; in January it may readily sink to —20°; add to the latter a middling gale and the chill factor plunges to —95° and points below. The atmosphere is thin, so dangerously thin that it may fail to filter ultraviolet radiation from the sun, and permit chlorophyll damage to plants and painful burns to humans.

That is all. For anyone hounded by enterprise, practicality and purpose, this ridge is a very useless place. It's also alien and can sometimes be downright mean.

But back around 1780 at a similar alpine site in Wyoming's Bighorn Range, native Americans of the Crow Nation placed an alignment of rocks in the shape of a great wheel—a Medicine Wheel 75 feet across with 28 radial spokes—for their ceremonial sun dance honoring and invoking the good will of their great god, giver of light, life and everlasting strength. And elsewhere in the Rockies other mountain sites are accorded equally sacred significance. Blue Lake high in the New Mexican reach of the Sangre de Cristo, its sapphire depths the source of all life for the people of the Taos Pueblo. Going-to-the-Sun Mountain in Montana's Glacier National Park where Napi, Old Man, god of the Blackfeet, came down from the sun to aid his people. Colorado's Pikes Peak; created by Manitou, Great Spirit of the Utes, who made a hole in the sky and poured through it a mountain of snow and ice.

A nameless, 13,150-foot ridge? Perhaps it is not so useless after all. Though the ridge is the site of no ancient ceremonies, the subject of no distant legends, it easily could be. And though such lore may be more foreign to many of us than Asia, its possibility, just one brief tale, is hard to set aside. Some say this universe is Godless, but it still can house its share of sacred places.

When I first saw the ridge I was a wide-eyed mountain greenhorn, a recent emigrant from the confinements of New England via the flatlands of southern Michigan. At the time I barely saw the ridge for below it lay a pair of blue, gem-like lakes and abutting it at the point of the fishhook two immense bonerock summits reaching well above 14,000 feet: Crestone Peak shaped like a giant cockscomb, and Crestone Needle appearing more like the prow of a sinking ship. Since Coloradans have bestowed a special significance on that 14,000-foot mark, I also carefully noted 14,064 Humboldt Peak, rising in the less imposing form of an overgrown anthill at the opposite end of the ridge. My stereotyped perception of these mountain sights occupied me almost totally; my mind was filled with swift, jubilant snapshots.

Only as I left the lower of the two lakes, first afoot, then jolting in my jeep down an old rock-studded wagon road, did I sense that my journey had been somehow incomplete. An outsider, I had gazed up at the peaks, had marvelled at their lofty beauty from various angles and distances. But that was all. I had not penetrated these mountains; I had not rummaged around or been immersed or really sunk in—and I had not truly felt.

Several months passed before I vaguely concluded that the ridge, especially its broad bench at the head of the cirque, might be the key to what I was after. Off and on that following winter I poured over my government contour map of the area—first aimlessly dreaming, later trying to figure a route up the ridge. By spring I'd devised a more furtive plan and as soon as the snows had melted I was back. My idea was to angle gradually up below Humboldt to the straight shank of the fishhook, then scramble along its rocky rim to my goal.

It didn't work.

Five hundred yards down the shank the ridge stopped. Nothing on my map prepared me for such a gap. I imagined a giant sword cleaving it in a swift, violent blow. The cut was deep, abrupt and impassible, and though the ridge resumed on the far side, the surrounding wreckage of loose rock made a detour unwise. Cautiously I picked my way back along the rim, then retreated to the lakes. On my second journey I'd come closer to my goal; the incompleteness of such a near miss only nagged worse than ever.

Two more years passed. This time my return coincided with an August afternoon storm which shrouded the Crestones and Humboldt in shifting billows of heavy mist. The ridge was there, too—appearing, vanishing and reappearing in the low clouds. At one point during the night, hail pelted my tent, and on several occasions, driving rain. But sometime during the dark, the clatter ceased and I dimly remember peering beneath the flap at a landscape flooded with full moonlight that drowned all but a scattering of the brightest stars.

I set off at dawn as the first pink light of the sun dropped onto the summit of Crestone Needle, then grew copper, yellow and almost blue as it edged down the peak's bulging northeast face. The first mile was an easy amble over the tundra as it rolled upward to the foot of the cirque. Tough on nothing but the lungs. This ended with a 60-degree scramble up the glacier scoured face always among loose rock (talus, scree) looking for firm rock, anything anchored to the solid inner core of the ridge. A handhold now. Then a foothold. Occasionally a place to sit, catch breath, rest legs, look around, gaze, dream.

Each time I stopped, I wondered if I'd make it. Seldom

could I see more than 50 feet ahead; beyond that, jutting rims and outcrops blocked my view. So I climbed piecemeal. A traverse across a rockslide, then stop and figure my next move. A scramble up a gravelly chute, then stop and figure again. Always with uncertainty, but at least the signs were good: no over slung ledges, no sheer walls. The four inches of slushy snow that had fallen during the night could be a problem; the higher I climbed, the less it had melted, but wait—there on that bare spot, what's that? An old footprint in a patch of sandy dirt; someone else has actually been here.

I assumed the maker of that Vibram track knew what he was doing; a seasoned mountaineer heading for the summit of one of the Crestones, maybe both. Whoever he was, he made me a believer, pumped me full of adrenalin and sent me vigorously on my way. Head down like a goat's, hands and feet wheeling in concert, I charged up the final 100 feet in a long, pell mell lunge.

One of the true joys of ratting about the mountains: you're never prepared for what greets you when you top a summit.

The bear went over the mountain,
The bear went over the mountain;
To see what he could see,
To see what he could see.

The proverbial other side is always more than you have imagined. It never matters that you've climbed that same peak, or ridge, or saddle many times before.

Sometimes it's just the glorious, madcap arrangement of peaks, their summits heaved, skewed and tilted wildly against the sky. Sometimes the ridge lines, slopes and valleys join in: their shadows, tones and textures. And often there's something else as well: a pattern of clouds (mottled sheepherder's clouds, a thin veil of cirrus, a column of thunderheads), a lifting storm, a rainbow, flickering lightening, a sunbathing marmot (he whistles and dashes for cover), dancing wildflowers, an unnamed lake, the slanting rays of the sun. Once in Colorado's San Juan Range when the wind blew in my face, I topped a ridge right into a herd of 25 or 30 elk; they flinched in unison, wheeled and ran. One of the larger bulls had lost an antler and wore a biologist's bright orange neckband.

No matter what: always a surprise, and so it was atop the fishhook-shaped ridge. The view plunged me back to those incredibly remote days not long after the stuff of this planet was flung from its parent, the sun: a scene of subterranean fires bursting through giant cracks in the cooling crust, of clouds of steam from vents, and seething gas and a brittle domed summit heaving and bobbing upward above the fiery, roiling mass.

Before me stood the fourth great 14,000 foot mountain in this reach of the Sangre de Cristo, Kit Carson Peak, once known by the more vivid and fanciful name of Haystack Baldy. The prevailing westerlies swept a low, dense wave of clouds against its flank which in turn deflected them upward like plumes of steam from a giant teakettle. Kit Carson's upper slopes seemed almost to float above the boiling, shifting swells as they gathered, then dissipated, then gathered again and enlarged in the bright morning sun (see page 51).

At first the air was calm, but soon a breeze picked up. To my south the sombre rock faces of the Crestones were still etched hard against a dark blue sky; to the northeast old Humboldt was bathed in glaring light. The clouds danced higher and higher round Kit Carson's three summit domes until these merged to a single, dim outline in a shroud of white. Then the peak vanished and the wind commenced to slap a fine horizontal rain in my face.

I stood there for close to a half hour. Let the clouds surround me and blot out first the Crestones, then Humboldt. Let the rain turn to hail, then back to rain and at last to more sticky snow. Let my whole body lean into the rising wind. Let the visibility shrink to 100, then 50, then 25 feet. Reached down and made a single, token snowball. Threw it into the thickening murk half expecting it to be flung back in my face. Stood. Listened. Heard nothing but the subdued roar of the wind. Then decided to beat it down off that beautiful, wild ridge while I could still see and feel what I was doing.

It is months later now; the memory of the ridge is fixed in my mind like a wedge. So is the desire to know it more. How really does one get deeper into the mountains? Next time shall I leave the ridge below and climb higher still? Up the west flank of Crestone Peak I have seen the tundra slanting above to 13,700 feet before giving way to raw rock. Or shall I simply stay longer on the ridge? Stay and sink in? Way in? I could pack tent, sleeping bag, extra clothes, food and stove up there and camp for several weeks.

Two whole weeks. An interval long enough to absorb the basic rhythms of the mountains—the hard, wild pulse of life on these uplifted masses of rock. A time to live by the rising and setting of the sun; to become accustomed to the absence of trees, to a vista that reaches 70 uninterrupted miles to the West and 25 or 30 to the East; to adapt to the whims and force of the mountain weather, the thin air, the bright sun, and at night the incredibly incandescent stars. A time for aimless wandering, poking about, watching, listening, sitting, climbing higher if I feel like it.

A fine, solitary sojourn if ever there will be.

I. THE GREAT RANGE

The Rocky Mountains are a land of many peaks, many ridges —as defined in this book, an immense, sprawling geographic province. Generally speaking every upthrust geologic mass between the end of the Great Plains and the beginning of the Great Basin belongs to the Rockies, and before that they belonged to the Stony Mountains (on some early maps) or the Shining Mountains (on others). Those were the old days — days before Lewis and Clark, before Zebulon Pike and Stephen Long, before the fur trappers and the overland caravans and Missouri River keelboats that served them — days when the Western mountains of the Louisiana Purchase by whatever name were mostly imagination and a modicum of fact: a single, awful, snowcrested wall rising three, four, even five miles vertically from the plains. And before that there were no Rockies at all and Columbus' legendary passage to India was a mere ten days' journey beyond the Alleghenies.

Neither logic nor reason scoped these mountains for in the march of American history, image inevitably preceded reality. When trailblazers spied the Black Hills over the waving tallgrass of the plains, they were the Rockies. The same was true of the Laramie Range in Wyoming, the Front Range in Colorado, the Sangre de Cristo in New Mexico, hundreds more. Only later were individual ranges singled out and given their own names, but by then it was too late: the Rockies were everywhere until you were well across Utah or clear into Oregon. All the mountains were part of them.

Some modern statistics: The Rockies reach north across the Canadian Yukon to Alaska, plunge deep into New Mexico, sinking at last to rippled, diminishing ridges south of Santa Fe. In the U. S. total area exceeds 250,000 square miles, and elevations vary by more than 13,000 feet. The region's official high point is Colorado's Mt. Elbert (a mammoth, dull lump surveyed at 14,431 feet); the unofficial low point is in Idaho where the western flanks of the westernmost range plunge into North America's deepest gorge, Hell's Canyon, with Oregon and Washington on the opposite side (height here drops under 800 feet). Idaho alone counts 81 named ranges, New Mexico 73 and Colorado a modest 34 if one doesn't list smaller spurs and off-shoots. The Continental Divide threads north-south through the Rockies, separating the Atlantic and Pacific watersheds; rains from a single summer shower along this wandering crest may with equal ease irrigate crops in California's Imperial Valley or burst levees in New Orleans.

Up in the mountains the climate is harsh; on the surrounding basins, plains and plateaus it is less harsh but uncompromisingly dry. An oasis civilization the region has been called and for this reason even today it is sparsely inhabited, the average for the six mountain states being only about ten people per square mile (or 64 acres per person). Almost every major city lies on a river and most of the lesser ones as well, Denver on the South Platte, Casper on the North Platte, Boise on the Snake, Great Falls on the Missouri, Albuquerque on the Rio Grande. No water: no town. The entire regional population is roughly equivalent to that of the United States in 1805 or that of Switzerland in 1970: about 6.4 million.

What the Rockies lack in people they make up for in magnificent natural diversity. First off, this region is an astonishing, exposed geologic showcase. The origins of the many ranges and the peaks within them include every major mountain building process known to geology; here are the aftermaths of folding, faulting, arching, of the inexorable drift of the earth's crustal plates, of varieties of volcanism. And here also are ample signs of mountain destruction: by glaciers; by heaving frost, running water, blowing particles, weathering.

Or if not rocks, then try plant life. Imagine a 2,500-mile overland journey from the Sonora of northern Mexico to north Canada's Polar Sea. Such a trek will lead you through an astonishing range of vegetation, beginning with the cactus and scrub of the high desert, ending with the tough, dwarfed world of the arctic tundra. A good year's march if done at a reasonable, leisurely pace. In the Rockies, increases in altitude take one on a similar trek. Do this in a single day—not everywhere, but wherever mountains rise sharply from lowlands: in central Colorado where Pikes Peak abruptly terminates the western edge of the Great Plains, in southeastern Utah where the La Sal Range bulks above the Colorado Plateau, in Hell's Canyon where you can see prickly pear blooming along the Snake River at dawn and, if you are in phenomenal shape, alpine buttercups in the Seven Devils Mountains before sunset. On the average, a climb of 1,000 vertical feet is equivalent to a northward advance of 300 miles.

The gardens of the continent on a single mountain. Start in the low foothills of a peak in Colorado; there you can find cane cactus and purple fruited pad cactus, both of which also thrive far south into Mexico. Hike higher to the moist montane forest and you may find the soft pink calypso orchid which grows equally well in Alaska's Matanuska Valley. And finally timberline and above. In late August look for the green trumpetlike bloom of the arctic gentian; the same species flowers in abundance on the stony slopes and mountain meadows in the Canadian Yukon.

What else? Back to the human element: of all the diversities rising off the Rockies, none give more pure, dizzy joy than the names. Some of these are vaguely suggestive, others exact; some gently lyrical, others uncouth and abrupt. Almost all would spin yarns, though in many cases the details are lost in the past. Some hint at solid, historic events; more reflect how these peaks struck men's minds, and how those minds, in whatever frame, responded to them.

Names of the ranges are grander and more decorous than those of individual peaks, gulches, avalanches, canyons and creeks. Pour over a common highway map and the words leap out like fragments of lost but dazzling poems. Beartooth and Sawtooth. Bitterroot and Tobacco Root. Wasatch and Sawatch. There are ranges named for the flowing waters that carve them: Salmon River, Lost River, Wind River, Bear River, Snake River. Ranges named for their wildlife: Bighorn, Beaverhead, Bearpaw, Elk, Mosquito, Swan. And for their minerals: Sapphire, Ruby, Garnet. Some bear names from the many tongues of the American Indian: Absaroka, Cochetopa, Rawah, Uinta, Washakie, Lemhi. Names bestowed by early Spanish conquistadores, monks and settlers: La Garita, San Juan, San Miguel, San Pedro, Sangre de Cristo. And crisp, descriptive names seeming no more than the result of a quick glance, a casual sizing up by a wandering fur trapper or rock struck sourdough: Crazy, Snowcrest, Rampart, Ten Mile, Smoky, Blue, Black.

But it is in the naming of individual sites that the dreams, madness, despair, humor and grit of pioneer times in the Rockies echoes most firmly. There are mountains such as Isolation, Singleshot, Flirtation, Bad Marriage, Dollarhide, Heavy Runner, Scarface, Bearhat and Mamma. Creeks named Coltkilled, Brokenback, Crazy Woman, Poison Spider, Arsenic, Bad Luck and Gloom. Gulches called Starvation, Dead Man, Waterloo, Poverty, Twobit and Hope. The Mother Cline, Blue Point, Shirttail and Slippery Jim avalanches skin down mountainsides near Ouray in southwestern Colorado; Sewemup Mesa rises just above Sinbad Valley further west near the Utah line. There is a trail called Horsethief, a lake known as Hell Roaring, a ridge named Skull. This is the true folk poetry of the Rockies: rough, earthy and atonal. Born mostly of the two great 19th century adventures in this region: the first to pull beavers from the streams that spilled from the mountains, the next to dig silver, or better, gold from the insides of the mountains themselves. The names are the living language of this land, the Rockies, and of survival, the posture into which all first comers were inevitably forced. If only we knew the tales and tragedies behind this hubbub of frontier names, the circumstances, the life stories, the evidence, the facts. If only that then no more histories would be needed.

But perhaps it is better that we are left with questions instead. Who was Mother Cline? Who wore a bearhat? Who ran heavily and why? Who made a single shot and what did he kill? What woman went crazy (and why), who was bit by a poison spider (and what happened to him), who starved and whose back was broken and how (did he fall from a horse or a cliff or get mauled by a grizzly)? Who had bad luck and what about (no pelts, no gold, plenty Indians, plenty snow)? Who flirted with whom to what effect? What hide was worth a dollar, who paid whom, and with what (trinkets, gunpowder, a blow in the head or coin)? Whose face was scarred, why was it scarred, and by what (an arrow, a knife, smallpox or the hoof of a mule)? Who was sewn up and how did Sinbad get into the Rockies?

Thus a few bits and pieces of the Great Range of which my nameless 13,150-foot ridge is a part. It is a region which no human can encompass. If any came close to that it would be one of the legendary mountain men: a Jim Bridger, a Tom

Lodgepole forest, Yellowstone National Park, Wyoming.

Fitzpatrick, a Joe Meek. They were ever on the move—trapping first one stream and then another, staying in one place only to hole up for the winter or attend the annual summer rendezvous and trade beaver pelts for another year's supplies. No miner travelled like this; he looked for the one, eternal place, site of the elusive bonanza, the vein that yielded nothing but high grade ore for a lifetime. He moved on only when the mines played out or failed to pay off in the first place.

But even the mountain men didn't encompass the Rockies. None thereafter have had either the opportunity or the necessary compulsion to do so.

II. MOUNTAIN TIME

There is no escaping time in the Rockies. Every mountain, canyon, gulch, wash and draw is an exposed geologic clock, partial to be sure but nevertheless a record of what is happening to this land. Or what happened, or didn't happen when it was roamed by mammoths and before that by stegosaurs, when it was washed by even earlier seas, baked by the old sun, heaved, buckled, blistered and before all a collapsing cloud of interstellar gas and dust: the raw matter out of which the solar system formed something over 4.5 billion years ago.

It takes a while for this realization to strike. The Rockies are both massive and beautiful. In my early days among them I often simply marveled at the vivid, impressionist scenes: the grand geometry of ridgeline and peak cutting the sky, the austere patterns of shadow and light, the bizarre summit shapes, chimneys, horns, pagodas, stovepipe and cockade hats; fo'castles and turrets, spires and domes. Later I started looking nearer and down at my feet as well as up, and so became intrigued with the ways of life of these mountains. When and why elk, with their lower teeth, strip bark from aspens. How forest fires can rejuvenate the land. Why porcupines are rough on pinon pines. Why wand lilies shouldn't be eaten (they are poison) and how monkey flower leaves make excellent salads.

The mountains unfolded in other ways, too, especially their human history. At the mouth of Carnero Creek where it sinks into southern Colorado's San Luis Valley, a friend showed me Indian pictographs, probably Ute, on a rocky face halfway up a cliff. Throughout the region at sites like Telluride, Garnet, St. Elmo, Custer and Sneffels, I explored the weathered husks, and active remnants, of old 19th century gold and silver camps. And one summer, chasing even earlier signs of man's days in the Rockies, I ended up not far from my ridge in the Sangre de Cristo.

As the hawk flies it is less than three miles, east by southeast, from the crest of the ridge to the summit of Marble Mountain. The peak itself is merely a swell on an easy alpine ridge, but down its eastward flank, at 11,550 feet, a deep cave has been eroded into the limestone, La Caverna del Oro it is called, the Cave of Gold. On a boulder near its mouth someone has painted an umber Maltese cross which is now faded and appears to be very old. Shadowy accounts date it in the 1600s, maybe earlier; they say it is the work of a Spanish monk, Fray Juan de la Cruz, or one of his men, and that somehow this cross marks the site of a hidden hoard which has never been found. These stories also tell, though with less confidence, that de la Cruz was not the first here: that he was only looting a lode where earlier Aztecs had also found gold which they offered to their frightful god Huitzilopochtli in the temple at Tenochtitlàn (later Mexico City).

Playing treasure hunter, I crawled into the horizontal entrance tunnel, roped along the edge of a terrifying black pit and slithered upward into a damp, limey jungle of rock where I found nothing but my own fear and an urgent desire to flee at an extremely rapid pace. In daylight again I hiked down from the entrance of this highest major cave in North America and in an aspen grove poked among log remains, possibly old crude breastworks, fronted by a series of what could once have been rifle pits.

Early settlers hereabouts claim to have found old arrowheads embedded in the logs of this rough fort, and deep in the cave above, more recent spelunkers have discovered the remains of a 17th century windlass. But part way between the two sites, in small chunks of limestone dislodged from the face of Marble Mountain, I stumbled across curious rocks which mocked the modernity of both. I had thought about geologic time in the Rockies before, especially on an afternoon in Wyoming's Gooseberry Badlands when I imagined myself scuba diving over the floor of an ancient sea, also the day I first saw dinosaur tracks in the red sandstone Dakota Hogback west of Denver. But somehow finding fossil crinoid stems at 11,000 feet on Marble Mountain forced the age of this land sharply into focus.

The crinoid was a beautiful, delicate marine creature, ancestor of the modern sea urchin, with 18 or 20 frondlike arms attached to the head of a long stalk anchored to the ocean floor. An animal that looked like a lovely underwater flower: living in vast, swaying colonies; languidly waving his arms to send slight currents of water to his mouth where tiny plants and animals were filtered for food. The crinoid lived when tepid Paleozoic seas washed the region 320 million years ago. He wasn't the highest form of life in his time, but he flourished ably and leisurely for an interval that dwarfs the human presence on this planet. And here he was, his impression, high and dry on the flank of a 13,226-foot Colorado peak well into the 20th century.

I slipped a small rock containing several of his fossil stems into my pack and went about my treasure hunting, but when I left Marble Mountain two days later, the crinoid was my only prize. What, I wondered, were life and the land like when he was alive? What had happened between his time and mine? Two summers later I asked similar questions in Montana's Glacier National Park as I hiked past stacked layers of ancient seabeds and beaches, multicolored limestones, mudstones and standstones, some over a billion years old, evenly deposited until they were over 13,000 feet thick. Then there was a trip into southern Wyoming's Snowy Range where I stumbled over a peculiar lump of rock which today resembles hardened folds of doughy batter. Later I learned these were fossil stromatolites: sediments trapped on a tidal flat by the slimy filaments of an algae that dominated life on this earth some 1.7 billion years ago. These are among the earliest organisms known; like the crinoids and some of Glacier's seabeds, they too had ended up more than 10,000 feet above our modern seas.

Imagine an impossible satellite orbiting for millenia at an Olympian vantage point in deep space above the Rockies. From that satellite, train a time-lapse camera toward this region and have it snap a single frame once every thousand years, accelerating as apt during episodes of unusually rapid geologic unrest. From such a perspective, one might begin to sense the intricate, ongoing mosaic of creation and destruction which has made the Rockies as they are today.

For an even sharper image, focus that camera on the site of

a single range, or a single summit—and watch what happens.

At 14,309 feet, Uncompahgre Peak (see page 15) is the highest peak in southwestern Colorado's San Juan Range—a region known to many as the "Switzerland of America." Nineteenth century explorers mistakenly believed this was the highest mountain in Colorado, and therefore in the American Rockies. Modern surveys have since dropped it to number six on the list, but its stark profiles remain intact; from various points of the compass, Uncompahgre Peak resembles a horn, a nubbin, a hulking fo'castle and a leaning tower. Climbers know the mountain as a "walk-up"; only able legs and lungs are required for the summit hike. But the peak holds another kind of danger; its metallic traces attract lightning and cause bizarre electrical phenomena. Rocks sizzle and snap like grease on a griddle, and an early climbing party reported their hair stood stiff on end like porcupine quills. In the late 1800s a miner's cabin clung briefly to the peak at 12,500 feet, but no gold came of his search. The name Uncompahgre is Ute for "hot water spring"; it derives from warm flows in a valley several miles west.

Those are a few recent facts, but the story of this peak begins far earlier: at a time when dinosaurs dominated the land; when ancestral beech, birch, oak and maple trees had made early appearances, and when forerunners of opossums, moles and shrews were the largest, fiercest and only mammals around. Before this peak existed there was still the site; its story is stretched to great length, sinking deep into the remotest recesses of time.

It is impossible to begin at the beginning; the evidence is either gone or indecipherable. But sometime around two billion years ago the first shadowy image in the Uncompahgre region appears: the dim outline of an ancient mountain range, uncertain in relief and vague in extent. What did it look like? We don't know. The deep, remnant core of these peaks is dark and hard, mostly gneiss and schist, among the oldest rock known to man. Otherwise, we know only that this Archean range was not hard enough to resist the ruin of time.

A billion years of erosion flicker before the eye: wind, rain, running water and blowing sand slowly grade the mountains until they are reduced to soft, rounded hills. Shallow seas lap against the lingering headlands, and at an annual rate of a millimeter or two, their rising waters slowly flood the region until not a patch of earth is to be seen for hundreds of miles. The site of Uncompahgre Peak is an ocean floor.

This time only 300 million years pass, time enough for grains and granules to settle to the sea bottom, layer after layer of dark sandstone and shale, until these are stacked over two miles thick.

Something like 700 million years ago, a welter of subterranean forces creates another picture here. Over a broad area the earth begins slowly to rise, pushing aside the seas and heaving a second generation of mountains against the sky. Great blocks of the earth's crust lift and wedge like trapdoors from the level land forming troughs and ridges which from bottom to top may measure 20,000 feet, the approximate height of Alaska's Mt. McKinley. It is an awesome, stark, barren landscape, devoid of living things for these have yet to emerge from the sea.

This second, severe, angular range is known as the Ancestral Rockies and it may well be more dramatic than the panoramas we know today. But it is far from timeless; even as the mountains rise, they are attacked by erosion, and after the uplift first slows, then ceases, they are reduced to geologic stumps, then vanish. Twelve thousand feet of sediment are stripped away; again the seas advance and sweep over this vast land.

Once more only ocean shows in the picture of the site where Uncompahgre Peak will appear. Enter crinoid; by his time a different geologic rhythm holds sway. For more than 400 million years no mountains build, but there is a gentler heaving; slowly inland seas rise and fall. The clock reads about 225 million years ago as one of these ebbs helps extinguish fully half the earth's families of marine life including every last lovely crinoid. This is the greatest mass dying known to evolution. The episode occurs quickly—several million years is all—but to the eye it is hardly noticeable, certainly not dramatic. The line of flotsam on the beaches of the receding seas is its only sign.

Dinosaurs dominate the land; the seas return for the final time and drive them elsewhere. But the pulse of the earth is insistent; inevitably the oceans retreat, and behind them they leave their normal legacy: more stacked layers of mudstone, sandstone, shale and marl, dry land once again, but for mysterious reasons no longer as hospitable for the dinosaurs who hold on briefly before enduring their own great dying.

Uncompahgre Peak is yet to be born, but now only 70 million years separate past and present. Slowly the San Juan country has begun to lift in a broad, arched dome—simple beginnings for a vast, complex episode that will give us the mountains we know today. As the dome continues to rise in a giant, earthen blister, local events join and accelerate this central mountain building force. Areas of the great welt fold and buckle upward; large blocks crack from their surroundings and independently rise. Near the peak, subterranean pressures blow a huge hole through the overlying crust which crashes in around it; to the south and west, other volcanoes are born—all blasting hot rock "bombs," cinders, ash and dust over the youthful mountain upland; often spilling out vast lava flows as well. Several of these eventually self-destruct in immense single explosions, scattering ejecta for miles in every direction. For 30 million years, the region throbs in a state of profound geologic unrest. There is erosion all this time, too; the solid cores of peaks seem to rise only to be buried, all but their upper thousand or two feet, beneath a sea of volcanic litter. For long intervals smoke covers the entire range. Even in quiescent times the atmosphere is clogged with particulate debris; the sun reduces to a dim, orange disc in a sky of perennial gray.

Before the cataclysm subsides the entire central and eastern San Juan are buried beneath layers of volcanic junk; among this is the substance of Uncompahgre Peak, but not its prominent, modern shape. The site belongs to a high plateau of lava, cinder and ash; the latter two fused and welded to a rock known as tuff. It is 40 million years ago and the mountains are young, immense and complete—complete in that they are relatively unsculpted, and exist in far greater bulk and height than we know today. In some places in the San Juan, elevations may well exceed 20,000 feet; on the slopes are lush tropical forests, and among the heavy growth, a younger race of creatures, the mammals, are evolving toward modernity. Among these interlopers: ancestral squirrels, burrowing beavers, short-faced dogs, early rabbits.

Now the final sequence. The higher the mountains, the swifter the erosion. In humid times, streams carve veinlike, V-shaped valleys north and south of the undifferentiated zone of rock soon to become Uncompahgre Peak. In drier ages, the rolling plateau is worn by wind and blowing particles. Slowly the image begins to assume familiar lines. Around the site of the peak, the high plain is whittled away, pared down, destroyed—and so a resiliant, rounded swell begins to bulk gently above the surrounding upland.

For some reason this swell is demolished more slowly than the neighboring terrain; gradually it comes to dominate the landscape, but it is still unrecognizable and anything but spectacular. Then, several million years ago, the first glaciers build out of the catchment basins, spread onto the alpine plain, and finally cold-fuse, head to head, across it. Now the whole range is mantled in a cap of ice, its glacial tentacles reaching far down the main valleys.

Long before this the general topography around Uncompahgre has been set; the glaciers grind along these established contours, planing away more of the plateau, carving and straightening the valleys below, but leaving the young peak generally intact. The ice retreats, but repeatedly it returns, six, eight, maybe a dozen times, each advance sharpening the relief of the land. Except on the southeast, Uncompahgre's gentler flanks are hewn completely away; its north slope is gouged to a vertical 1,200-foot face. Only the swell's core is left, a rocky remnant rising far above the eroded plateau.

As they do to every major range in the Rockies, glaciers apply all but a few of the finishing touches. Subsequent erosion by wind, water and weathering add these refinements. The softer tuff breaks down faster than the layers of hardened lava; the slopes take on a stair-stepped appearance, and from my favorite vantage point the larger peak dwindles to the shape of a magnificent, hulking fo'castle.

Change a few details in this story—or add, or subtract—and this is also the story of every summit and range in the Rockies from Montana to New Mexico. The San Juans differ only in their complexity; the range is a province of extreme, diverse geologic unrest. Wyoming's Yellowstone Plateau and the adjacent Absaroka Range are also immense volcanic dumps, but their rock has not been racked and twisted, folded and faulted like that of the San Juan. The tumbled mountain maze of the vast Idaho Primitive Area has an equally easy story; once it was a sprawling subterranean welter of molten rock which forced its way upward beneath old stacked sea beds only to cool hard before it could explode into the air; this mass became visible only after softer overlying sediments were eroded away. The Sangre de Cristo near my ridge is a comparatively simple fault-block uplift, devoid of volcanic complications. Likewise Wyoming's magnificent Tetons, youngest range in the entire Rockies.

Try one more imaginative leap and compress the entire story of this region into a single, properly proportioned day. Watch the events flash past.

The first twelve hours from an instant past midnight, to dawn, to noon are essentially blank. None can reconstruct what happened during that long, incredibly ancient interval. But shortly thereafter the Archean Rockies begin to rise, and around 1:00 P.M. faint green algae first appears in the neighboring seas. By 5 P.M. the first mountains are completely gone. The Ancestral Rockies appear around 9:20 P.M. and disappear before 10:00. The last crinoids die out before 11:00, but the modern Rockies don't start to lift until about 11:47—their birth being roughly a ten-minute phenomenon.

Down to the final minutes. At approximately 150 seconds before midnight the first great glaciers begin to scour the Rocky Mountains; the last ice doesn't recede until the final second. Early in this same interval man begins to evolve in an African gorge; much later he wanders across the Bering Straits land bridge into the Western Hemisphere. The Paleo-Indian known as Folsom man isn't hunting long-horned bison in northern New Mexico until 1/10 of a second before this incredible day's end. And finally, at something like 1/250 of a second before midnight, one Francisco Vásquez de Coronado leads a weary, disheartened troop of Spaniards north beyond Mexico. These are the first Europeans to gaze on the Rockies. They see and cross the New Mexican reach of the Sangre de Cristo; in so doing, they toll the beginnings of the modern era of this land.

So it is today, but only today.

Uncompahgre Peak is already a remnant; likewise every other summit, ridge and range in the Rockies. We know the inexorable levelling will continue as future events compress into the earth's long day. Wind, sand, water and ice will surely perform this destruction; we don't know the sequence it will take, only that, on some distant day the stuff of the modern Rockies will be reduced to an ultimate featureless plain.

Mountains only give the illusion of permanence, reassuring as that illusion may be; like everything else on this planet they are in process, in the case of the Rockies a process of dying, in slow geologic time.

INTERLUDE: THE ALPINE WORLD

For 24 years the University of Colorado's Institute of Arctic and Alpine Research (INSTAAR) has maintained a climate-monitoring station atop Niwot Ridge at 12,300 feet in the Front Range above the city of Boulder. Like my ridge in the Sangre de Cristo, the site is far above timberline; in a rough and ready way, it typifies the high world of the Rockies.

Take an average year during this period; INSTAAR's data provides a cold, clear picture of what life can be like at such heights. Normally Niwot Ridge will witness only about 45 frost-free days annually with summer "ending" toward mid-August; wind-swept, wet sites are underlaid by permafrost. Like that of Nome, Alaska, mean temperature is 26 degrees F; high during these 24 years was 67.5, low —34. Wind velocity averaged a brisk 18 miles an hour and on some 20 days each year it topped 100 mph. Rains fall over 40 inches annually, over 250 inches of it snow, most of it blowing to deeper drifts in valleys below. On 20 or so days a year, the humidity drops below a dessicating 10 percent.

In lower mountain valleys around 9,000 feet, one is out of the worst of the incessant wind and has a longer growing season. However, the temperature normally plummets wherever the terrain collects and traps cool air masses. Colorado's premier icebox is Taylor Park, a broad valley tucked in a bend of the Sawatch Range near the center of the state. Elevation here is 9,500 feet, record low temperature an even —60° achieved on February 1, 1951.

The mountains are not an easy world and three additional factors make them even less so. First: while slopes vary from gentle to sheer, they are commonly precarious, often a hazard or barrier. Except for a few species that have evolved special means of coping with such steepness, life is more at home on the flat. Second: soils are shallow to nonexistent. Short growing seasons and diminutive plant growth slow the building of humus. Third: winter avalanches can make mountainous terrain dangerous in a swift, fatal way. Killer slides snap full grown trees like matchsticks and, despite all precautions, claim a steady number of human lives annually. Large avalanches have rocketed down mountainsides at speeds up to 200 miles an hour; their force has been measured at over 45 tons per square yard, and they may pack as hard as Portland cement, thereby immobilizing most victims who then die of suffocation. Some might wish to add altitude to this list (it does make some people ill), but most forms of life can adapt.

Living in the mountains is not done in a quest for comfort and ease. As you ascend the tiers of life zones, this impression becomes unmistakeably clear: life chooses increasingly greater heights with steadily growing reluctance. In the great middle elevation montane forests, bristlecone, whitebark and limber pines are often crowded out by more aggressive trees, so these species flee upward for survival — upward to timberline to eke out a wind-twisted cold-stunted existence away from competitors. Many varieties of plants grow smaller and more compact as elevations increase; in the foothills west of Denver I have seen Indian paintbrush growing several feet high on long, branched stems; on the alpine tundra, this common wildflower may be full grown at two or three inches.

Before the modern Rockies began to rise there was no need for such desperate adaptations. But as land lifted its life to greater heights, new forms had to evolve, at first almost lazily, later more rapidly because of the cooling climate and eventually the many glacial advances. Paleobotanists figure today's alpine tundra is the earth's youngest major ecosystem. But anything more than its approximate age is hard to come by; ever deteriorating mountaintops are ill suited surface areas for fossil preservation.

The world above treelimit isn't something to get used to overnight. Hike upward through the montane and subalpine forests where trees often reach well above 100 feet, cross that austere boundary known as timberline, wander onto the tundra — and suddenly you become an oversized Gulliver. Scale and perspective are tossed on end, and the only way to set matters aright is to drop to your knees for a close-up look. If you've a hand lens, so much the better.

A sunflower full grown at six inches (see page 70), a willow mature at two, a forget-me-not at less than that. Pygmy buttercup, sandwort, alpine candytuft and rock jasmine, all of them lovely wildflowers, none of them larger than a penny. Above all this is a dwarfed world: dwarfed to the sole end of survival through conservation and sheer self-defense.

Small size cuts down on exposed surfaces; this helps reduce evaporation in the dry mountain climate and keeps a plant from desiccating to a crisp (a standard oak leaf would bake on the tundra). Small size also protects against the buffeting wind; many alpine flowers huddle in low mats or cushions (a long stalk would snap in the first hard blow). Most important of all, small size conserves; in this cold world large leaves and long stems would waste vital energy which must be saved for seed production and for those perilous early spring weeks when photosynthesis is uncertain.

Thus the economies of small scale on the mountain tundra; they are vital but far from the only strategies needed to survive in such a severe realm. To assure a steady supply of water, the moss campion (see page 182) may sink a long taproot six feet deep—an adaptation which doubles as an anchor in areas of frequent frost heaving. Some tundra species have evolved fuzzy, hairlike coatings on their leaves to diffuse the intense alpine light and also the steady wind. Most fascinating of all is the manner in which alpine plants grow. With a lone exception, all 300 or so Colorado species are perennials; the high mountain summer is too brief for a complete life cycle in a single year. Instead these gritty little flowers do their growing in cautious stages: stems and leaves one summer, nascent buds the next, blossoms not until the third.

For a confirming perspective on the alpine world, look at those hardy few animals who dwell year round in this land above the trees. The pika (or cony, or rock rabbit) is a perennial, pint-sized denizen of the high mountain talus piles, and a marvel of alpine adaptation. Zoologists recognize him as a legitimate rabbit, a lagomorph they say, but to the casual observer he looks more like a chubby hamster; his tail is a vestige, ears round and compact, legs short. All this to the sole end of energy conservation; body mass is great, while extremities have shrunk to cut back heat loss. This arrangement is precisely opposite that of the antelope jackrabbit, desert cousin to the pika, who developed his long vessel-lined ears to dissipate heat (relocate him on the tundra and he would soon die of exposure or jackrabbit hypothermia). Unlike most of his kin, the pika is also a noisy little fellow; since stubby legs limit his ability as a runner (a rabbit's normal means of fleeing predators), he has developed a bleating, warning squeak (when one pika sounds the alarm, all within hearing scoot for cover among the rocks).

And never forget this entire alpine world is wonderfully woven together. On the tundra rocks there grows an orange lichen that thrives only on pika urine; watch for orange lichen and you may well discover a pika den or lookout point. Lichen in turn is a pioneer species growing where nothing else will, on unbroken rock; it secretes acids and sends out filaments which slowly break down that rock, eventually helping produce new soil which will grow new grasses to feed new pikas. Also, another remarkable adaptation: the pika's urine is crystalline, a trait to help him combat dehydration in the dry mountain air.

Other mountain wildlife show similar adaptive quirks. The ptarmigan is chunkier than most grouse, grows feathers about its feet for warmth, and will hole up in its own rudimentary snow caves at night or during a storm. The marmot (see page 19), mountain cousin to the Eastern woodchuck, is an outstanding hibernator; during his deep winter's sleep, his body temperature drops to the freezing point, his heart beats only once every ten or 15 seconds, and he breathes at four or five minute intervals. The Rocky Mountain bighorn sheep has evolved a blockier body than most ungulates, spongy underhoofs for surer traction on rock, and bones of extreme tensile strength to withstand the shock of jolting leaps.

Other wildlife in the high country is seasonal. Deer, elk, coyotes, eagles, hawks: all and many others may ply the ridgetops in the summer, or float on the air currents veering off them. But come fall and their time in this lofty world is up. Animals migrate lower, birds fly south. All instincts for survival signal retreat.

Were man ruled by instincts of such unswerving soundness, he would do likewise. Come winter, the alpine world is not his province, not even when he dons the many protective adaptations he has so ingeniously devised. Down parka, hood and bivouac pants are stopgaps; likewise high altitude sunglasses, layers of woven wool, expedition tents and all the other paraphernalia of the modern snow mountaineer. This gear allows him to be considered a very capable visitor, but hardly a steady resident.

Snow he can handle, albeit with difficulty, and also deep cold, high winds and blinding sun. But avalanches are another story. In January 1975 alone, scientists at INSTAAR's San Juan research unit observed 327 slides—84 of them reaching a well traveled U. S. Highway—and estimated some 3,000 in this one range. Avalanches closed down mountain mines and blocked roads; they put snowplow crews on 24-hour alert, and claimed eight skiers in Colorado including one experienced hand I counted as a friend, not close, but one I'd hoped to know better. None will ever know what actually happened to Art Evans. One can only imagine the sudden gust of wind, the muffled roar and wall of white, the surge and desperate effort to ski out, the tumbling over and over losing all sense of which way is up. And finally the entombed stillness, serenity succeeding violence as if nothing had happened at all. A lone searcher found my friend beneath only 15 inches of snow, one hand reached out into the ever so dependent life-giving air.

The towering Rockies give us humans ample reason for hating them and forever leaving them alone; we requite this with yearning and love.

Thanksgiving Day, 1806. Sockless, dressed only in light cotton and without food for two days, U. S. Army Lieutenant Zebulon Montgomery Pike gazed on the Colorado peak that bears his name and wrote in his journal: "I believe that no human being could have ascended to its pinical." The American imagination seized his words from context (Pike was merely assessing his party's chance of a successful climb as it stood 16 miles from his peak in three feet of snow recording the temperature at —4 degrees) and turned them into an irrefutable myth of an invincible mountain which it then proceeded to conquer with a vengeance. The myth refused to die when three men walked to the summit in July 1820, when a cog railway rattled up the peak in 1890, when Katherine Lee Bates was inspired to write the beginnings of "America the Beautiful" atop the mountain in 1893, when a group of Colorado Springs brahmins promoted a whiplash of an automobile road up the Peak in 1916, or when Bobby Unser, driving a Dodge Dart "kit car" powered by a 461 hp Chrysler engine, won the 52nd annual Pikes Peak Auto Hill Climb in 1974 (breaking his own record by 26.9 seconds). Zeb Pike hadn't really said his peak was unclimbable; but America had decided it was and then couldn't stand such a humbling notion.

The Rocky Mountains, especially their alpine world, are another country—certainly not suitable habitat for the very beings who have swarmed all over them anyway. There are things alluring among these peaks far stronger than cold, a puff of wind or a hard blast of snow.

III. MOUNTAIN MAN

During one of the latter glacial advances the great ice sheets locked up so much moisture that the level of the earth's oceans dropped some 300 feet, and because of this, a land bridge many hundreds of miles wide was left across the Bering Straits between Siberia and Alaska. Over it wandered a long, loose migration of small tribes and bands following the tracks of the large animals which sustained them. Precisely when they arrived in the Western Hemisphere is still a question, maybe as early as 25,000 B.C. But even if they moved camp only three or four miles annually which is a plausible pace for such a migration, these peoples had plenty of time to reach the Straits of Magellan, southernmost tip of the Americas, no later than 8,000 years ago.

Certainly these groups passed by the Rockies and we know that some stayed. George McJunkin, a seasoned, inquisitive cowboy, accidentally found the first sign of these early Americans on a spring afternoon in 1925; he was tracking stray range cattle when his eye hung on a strange knob of bone jutting from the eroded bank of an arroyo. He forgot the cows, stopped to inspect and found more bones and a finely fluted flint projectile point, neither like any he'd ever seen. When archaeologists followed, they excavated the remains of 23 long-horned bison extinct for 10,000 years and more spearheads. The town of Folsom was nearby so the maker of these weapons became known as Folsom man; in the years since, his campsites have been found erratically throughout the Rockies, as have those of his predecessors, Clovis and Sandia man (along with bones of mammoths, giant ground sloths, prehistoric camels).

Aside from their wits, these early ones wielded two basic weapons: fire and the spear. Fire was a major instrument for hazing herds of buffalo over cliffs, the most effective way to hunt these animals before the Spanish reintroduction of the horse in the 16th century. Many buffalo jumps (as these cliff sites are known) have recently turned up, two of the most notable near Bozeman, Montana and Douglas, Wyoming. Some date back for millenia; others were in use when the first Americans were arranging themselves into the tribes, territories, allegiances and hostilities the first westward and northward wandering Europeans would encounter as they probed the blank spaces of an unknown continent they already claimed as their own.

Well before now the earth's neat time frame begins to expand, then cracks wide open; from the imaginary satellite, the camera starts clicking furiously. Individual centuries, decades, years, days, minutes become important. A new perspective reaches the Rockies. Written history arrives.

1276: the Indians of Mesa Verde in Colorado, who had lived for centuries in clear view of the southern Rockies, the La Plata Range, begin slowly to leave their elaborate stone cliff dwellings and sun temples.

1540: Francisco Vásquez de Coronado, Viceroy of Nueva Galicia, finds the peoples of New Mexico and eastern Arizona living in large pueblo towns similar to those at Taos and Acoma today. He is the earliest modern dreamer to gaze over this land. He searches for the Seven Cities of Cibola; when they materialize as post-Stone Age communities without gold he presses onward, east through the panhandle country into Kansas looking for the legendary Quivira which is bogus, doesn't exist at all.

1742: The French brothers Vérendrye, Pierre and Chevalier, trappers of the *voyageur* strain, see the Black Hills (or maybe the Big Horn Range, or the Laramie; records are vague), and certainly meet the Mandans and other high plains tribes. They are the first Europeans to approach the main Rockies.

1776: Escalante and Dominguez, good Spanish Friars, skirt Colorado's San Juans and several of Utah's ranges on a futile search for the road to Monterey; their starting point, Santa Fe, was also where they concluded their tour.

1806-1807: Zeb Pike and 23 green volunteers grope a bemused snake of a course across the plains, then through or around Colorado's Front, Sawatch and Sangre de Cristo Ranges before ending up captives of the Spanish governor in Santa Fe. Pike's official order on this mission was to discover the source of the Red River; his failure was total and because of this he has long since been reviled as "the lost pathfinder." However, the fault lies first with Pike's map, and only secondly with his slavish inclination to follow it. That map is an earnest and erroneous pastiche of the best information and fondest hopes available at the time, sketched by the German scientist Alexander von Humboldt (the 14,000-foot peak near my ridge in the Sangre de Cristo now bears his name). To Pike's misfortune, it shows the Red River rising in the Rockies rather than its true source in Texas. Small wonder that he boxes the compass, discovers the headwaters of the Yellowstone River in central Colorado (today these are in northwestern Wyoming), and returns East via Chihuahua under Spanish escort.

Humboldt's map, and many others drawn under the same spell only underscore the immense space of the Rockies, and the difficulties the vision of a young, expanding nation had in coping with it. Long after these mountains ceased to be a blank spot on the early maps, they remained a Byzantine maze. Cartographers located Santa Fe at both the head and mouth of the Missouri River. Still dreaming of Columbus' passage to India, they connected the Rio Grande and Colorado Rivers in a continuous watery path to the Pacific, or marked a channel joining the Great Salt Lake and San Francisco Bay (the River Buenaventura this was called), or maybe an easy 20-mile portage from the Missouri to the Columbia. It was acceptable to compress the Rockies, the Sierras and the Cascades to a single, massed range, and to sketch California as an island floating somewhere off the coast of Utah.

Lewis and Clark headed west to the Pacific two years before Pike, but their final expedition journal wasn't published until some months later. It succeeded in placing large parts of Montana and Idaho near their modern configuration, but a simple half-sentence in Lewis's first report to President Jefferson did more; these mountains, he wrote are "richer in beaver and otter than any country on earth." Though the returning trailblazers passed 11 separate fur trapping parties beating up the Missouri, it was these words that effectively convinced youthful America of the Rocky Mountain beaver and thereby led to the first full charting of this great unknown.

A mature mountain beaver may weigh up to 60 pounds; he has long front teeth, a flat tail, exceptional skill as a dam builder and a strong preference for a single mate. Also: the hairs of his thick, insulating underfur are minutely barbed, and near the root of his tail are two pod-shaped sacs containing a pungent glandular perfume known as castoreum. These last two traits made the Rocky Mountain fur trade possible, providing first its market, then its method. The tiny barbs made beaver pelts unexcelled for fashionable felting (especially for tall, stove-pipe hats), while the smelly "medicine" was the trapper's favorite beaver bait.

Capitalizing on sartorial whims, French *voyageurs* and Britons in the employ of the ruthless Hudson's Bay Company had traded and trapped their ways across Canada to the Pacific by 1810, but few of them probed south into the American Rockies, none extensively. That challenge fell to the three or so thousand men who from 1807 to 1842, pushed west from St. Louis to pursue the mountain beaver south of the 49th parallel. Mountain men they were called and they were the most astonishingly self-reliant breed this nation has ever produced. The ultimate frontiersman, loner, wanderer 600 miles from the nearest settlement: the distilled image of freedom in a new, wide-open land. The Western archetype: a befringed, buckskinned, moccasined American Adam footloose on his own in the harshest Eden so far discovered by his young republic.

The first temptation is to measure a man by his accomplishments and those of the mountain men were many. In their heads, if not on paper, they mapped the entire reach of the Rockies, filling in the blank spaces of this land, unraveling its vast maze. In the winter of 1807-1808, expatriate Virginian John Colter set off afoot on an 800-mile scouting jaunt through northwestern Wyoming, and so became the first white to bring back reports of the geysers, hot springs and bubbling mud pots of the Yellowstone region. In early 1824 Jedediah Smith, Thomas Fitzpatrick, James Clyman and others forged a trail across a low divide south of Wyoming's Wind River Range; this was the famous South Pass, and beginning two decades later thousands of covered wagons and foot weary emigrants would cross it en route to Oregon. That same fall, Jim Bridger drifted a bullboat down the serpentine Bear River to discover Utah's Great Salt Lake. Over a period of years, Kit Carson and his Taos trappers worked and helped name many of the streams in Colorado.

These are textbook accomplishments; the greater marvel of the mountain man is that he survived and thrived in this formidable land, that he acquired and mastered an array of wilderness skills with an expertise unequalled before or since. First of all, Jim Bridger and his kin needed the ability to cope with the raw mountain environment and everything it threw at them from drought to grizzlies to snow-blindness; that was easy and the craft of catching beaver was part of it (today whole books are written on trapping which is acknowledged as a "dying art"). The sheer physical demands were immense: you had to be able to carry a 200-pound pack on your back 400 miles and make the trip in two or three weeks. You couldn't get seriously sick; only an occasional hangover at rendezvous and a touch of rheumatism from all that wading in icy beaver ponds were permissible. If wounded, you'd better heal quickly and well (for three years Bridger plied his trade with a Blackfoot arrowhead, iron and hooked at the point, lodged in his lower back).

The mountain man had to hunt or gather, dress and cook all his food. He provided his own transportation, his own weaponry and his own equipment, all of which he had to use proficiently and service on the spot. He was his own physician and surgeon; he made his own clothing, built his own shelter, and procured the raw materials for both. Fluency in sign language was another requisite, or better yet, the ability to speak Crow, Shoshone, Arapahoe, Ute, Blackfoot, Flathead and Nez Perce well enough to engage in complex ritual exchanges. When dragged into an unfriendly village, you had to know whom to flatter, how to flatter him, what to trade, when to trade it, what spirits to invoke and their proper order—the object being to talk your captors out of taking your life. Likewise, you had to barter properly and decorously for a squaw-wife, and it also helped to know what to say to her after your wedding. On the other hand, the King's English could slide to patois, and what we call literacy was only a frill (Bridger fared well signing his name as "X").

A well rounded mountain man could, as the occasion demanded, be ruffian, murderer, liar, diplomat, conniver, cutthroat competitor and long-winded spinner of tales both tall and baroque (thus Bridger's yarn of a locale where petrified birds sang petrified songs in petrified trees; even gravity was petrified, he maintained).

Perhaps most important of all, the mountain man had to be an extraordinary reader of signs. This is historian Bernard de Voto's observation; here is how he probes the working of the trapper's ever alert senses and mind:

A branch floats down a stream—is this natural, or the work of animals, or of Indians or trappers? Another branch or a bush or even a pebble is out of place—why? On the limit of the plain, blurred by a heat mirage, or against the gloom of distant cottonwoods, or against an angle of sky between branches or where hill and mountain meet, there is a tenth of a second of what may have been movement—did men or animals make it, and, if animals, why? Buffalo are moving downwind, an elk in an odd area or posture, too many magpies are hollering, a wolf's howl off key—what does it mean?

Miss nothing: that was the unwritten law of the mountain man's life—all day, every day. And also: know what every sign means in an instant.

The Rockies, their denizens and the vicious intricacies of the fur business demanded all these skills—each refined, all finely meshed. Flunk any one and you were broken or dead or both. Pass them all and you didn't make much money, because the companies and the traders raked most of it off.

Heroic eras come and go quickly. By the late 1830s, the fur trade was moribund; the shewder mountain men would soon turn to guiding emigrants, scouting for soldiers, managing posts and forts. The bottom was dropping out of the fur market (silk hats were the new rage) and the beaver were thinned from overtrapping. But in less than four decades, a dogged, resourceful breed had become a legend and opened a land. Covering this, the mountain men covered the Rockies as none have done since.

Now others could follow, and they did, though most of them wished only to avoid the high country. Pioneers, missionaries, then 49ers, and still more pioneers trekked the Oregon Trail through increasingly hostile Indians, debilitating alkalai, bitter storms and diminishing buffalo. But not up into the mountains. The Pony Express, the transcontinental telegraph, the major stage and wagon routes, the transcontinental railroad: all did likewise. Prior to May 1859, when Georgia sourdough John Gregory drove his pick into a glittering vein of gold in the foothills west of Denver, only a few nontrappers, most in military uniform, entered the shining mountains.

Back in 1820 Major Stephen H. Long led an understaffed scientific expedition across the great plains and within distant view of the high Colorado peak that bears his name; then the group veered south where four of the party climbed Pike's great mountain and unknowingly logged the first ascent of a major summit in the Rockies. Two and a half decades later Brevet Captain John Charles Frémont marched to the mountains seeking a direct wagon or rail route across the Rockies. Reaching Wyoming's South Pass on his first journey, the flambuoyant "Pathfinder" truly a mathematical genius, could not resist an unauthorized side trip into the Wind River Range and another high summit. "We had climbed the loftiest peak in the Rocky Mountains," he wrote, "and standing where never human foot had stood before, felt the exultation of first explorers." Frémont then named the peak after himself.

Over 50 summits in the Rockies are higher than Frémont's and some of Benjamin Bonneville's trappers may well have climbed his peak 20 years earlier. No matter: Frémont's pronouncements had the promoter's convincing ring. All told he had four pioneering expeditions around and through the Rockies; his lofty and compelling reports on these treks were his great contribution (a less rhetorical soul would have had a much diminished effect). Though he was promoting himself for President, and not the mountain ambience, and though one of his parties spent a tragic winter in Colorado's San Juan Mountains (12 of his 36 men froze to death), he insisted the mighty and majestic Rockies could be enjoyed, revered and, most basic of all, crossed.

"The glowing pages of Frémont's tour to the Rocky Mountains in 1842-43," wrote 17-year-old Cincinnati schoolboy Hector Lewis Garrard, "were so alluring to my fancy that my parents were persuaded to let me go westward." And off he went, properly provisioned with letters of credit, cash, a pocket Bible, a rifle and a few calico shirts."

Successful promotion has always depended on skillful omission. The chilling, hard luck experience of most mountain miners could have damped this optimism, but tales of gold and dreams of wealth took over where Frémont's persuasiveness left off. Colorado's Front Range was first to be overrun, but the action soon spread north and south, fueled by hardened prospectors on the rebound from despair in California and Nevada, by owl-eyed Eastern greenhorns, by a diverse retinue of prostitutes, pimps, gunslingers, fugitives, con-men, gamblers and a hard working majority known as "the stable element."

Boom town is the common term for this phenomenon, and they materialized in a sequence of human explosions up and down the entire reach of the Rockies. Central City, Front Range, Colorado; incorporated 1859. Virginia City, Tobacco Root Range, Montana; 1863. Idaho City, Boise Basin, Idaho; 1864. South Pass City, southern Wind River Range, Wyoming; 1865. Park City, Wasatch Range, Utah; 1872. Silverton, San Juan Range, Colorado; 1874. Aspen, Elk Range, Colorado; 1880. Cripple Creek, behind Pikes Peak, Colorado; 1891.

These Rocky Mountain boom towns were also rip-roaring civic institutions whose growth followed an unerring, headlong pattern. First a few wandering prospectors; then a promising strike; then a cluster of drafty log cabins; then a saloon which doubled as a general merchandise store (also variously a gaming hall, hotel, stage station, eatery and brothel). Next came a post office which was very important. If the U.S. Government considered a place suitable for mail delivery, then it was also suitable to become an official town, or better yet, to be named "City," for that is what Western boosters have always wanted their settlements to become.

Other formalities followed. A townsite was surveyed and lots offered for sale. Incorporation was voted by the inhabitants (male only, save in Wyoming where women gained the vote in 1869, the first state in the U. S. where they were to do so); a church was built and a school; one or more newspapers cranked up; mills and smelters began rumbling away; the narrow gauge railroad arrived (much commotion and hoopla as the last spikes were driven); marshals and their deputies were elected.

What astonishes most about all this is the pace which was frenetic. Virginia City, Montana grew from zero to 10,000 in a single summer: from a wild, alder-lined gulch to a 17-mile strip of cabins, tents, dugouts and lesser shelters. When South Pass City, Wyoming reached age two, it counted six general stores, three butcher shops, five hotels, two breweries, a wholesale liquor establishment, dozens of saloons and "sporting houses," two livery stables and seven blacksmiths, one of whom practiced dentistry on the side. Gold and silver made men hurry and behind these metals was the rags-to-riches dream already well inflamed in the American mind. In 1869 Tom Walsh, illiterate son of an Irish farmer, emigrated to the U. S.; in 1895 he was searching for flux to be used in a smelter in Colorado's San Juans and instead found telluride quartz-gold in some old mine dumps on Canyon Creek above the town of Ouray; when he sold his mine in 1902, Walsh was a millionaire and had given his wife the Hope Diamond. Instances like this fueled the promise and refined the frenzy of the rapid stampede to the Rocky Mountains; success was more a matter of luck than skill, but luck has always held a peculiar power to inspire hope.

As always, a few struck it rich, many failed and most managed a living. In 1888 the Rev. J. J. Gibbons became the first

Warrior Ridge and Pingora, Wind River Range, Wyoming.

pastor of St. Patrick's Catholic Church in Ouray. Unlike most miners who were too busy to write much down, Father Gibbons left behind a charming, lucid memoir, *In the San Juan: Sketches,* to honor the spirit of his peers. He was a warm, matter-of-fact man who endured extreme hardships simply because they were there and he had a job to do. Gibbons was persistent in serving two parishes plus 20 missions and stations, all in the mountains. He was thankful when fellow passengers roped him out of the Uncompahgre River gorge (see page 17) after his sleigh overturned, was direct about a bitter February hike over 13,000-foot Virginus Pass to neighboring Telluride to read the last rites for a miner named Flannigan, was cheerful in recounting the companionship of a hunting trip for deer and grouse. Unlike the trappers, the people of the mine camps had to stand fast and slug it out with the worst of the high mountain winters—some losing to avalanches, bitter cold and deep snow; many more sticking to their obscure, backbreaking tasks—then blowing it off in town when given the chance. Too much is made of the seamy rowdiness of the camps; all in all the miners were a good, generous lot. As Father Gibbons said at the grave of his friend and parishioner, Billy Maher, a hard-working miner who died several days after eight sticks of dynamite exploded in his hands, "his life was more eloquent than any sermon I could preach." A trifle overstated for the larger gang, but the general drift is right.

The beavers ran out and the fur market collapsed; the mineral deposits merely ran thin, always with the promise of a rich vein just beyond the next stroke of the pick, and the market for gold and silver has, with vicissitudes, held. Today Tom Walsh is long since dead and the Hope Diamond is on another circuit, but his Camp Bird Mine still grinds away, as do a number of others in the Rockies. The goal of the miner was firmly rooted to a more solid stratum of the American republic than ever the haul of the fur trapper. In addition to creating towns, he also caused the building of wagon roads, railroads and supply centers. From the infinitesimal perspective known as the present, his impact is the first that can be called permanent. Many of his original camps still stand; more, however, are weather-beaten remnants: ghost towns, mines, headframes, boarding houses, shacks. Despite their tattered appearance (or, more likely, because of it), these are now among the most colorful traces of human history in the modern Rockies.

The mountain people who followed in the years since have been almost exclusively seasonal. Loggers, sheepherders, government trappers, hunters, guides, outfitters, backpackers, mountaineers, skiers, snowplow operators, avalanche rangers. At one time of the year, or another, the Rockies have beat back or disinterested all but a few 20th century challengers.

Only now is this situation beginning to change.

IV. THE PROSPECT

When the Rocky Mountain fur trade hit bottom, Jim Bridger, mountain man *par excellance,* wisely adapted: first he built a trading post for emigrants along the Oregon Trail; later he served a long stint as guide and scout for the U. S. Army. He was "Old Man Bridger" when they finally mustered him out in 1868—age 64, having spent 46 of them in the Rockies. His shoulders were stooped, his hair grayed, his black powder Hawken rifle sold and, ironically, the eyes which had seen so much so well so long were failing. He returned East to his daughter's Missouri farm where blindness overtook him.

And so our last image of this man: refusing to go out in a rocking chair on the veranda; instead riding a gentle gelding named "Ruff" about the family woods and farmlands in a small re-enactment of his great days in the Rockies. When he became lost, the horse knew the way home.

"I wish I was back in the mountains again," he once told a neighbor. "You can see so much farther in that country."

Bridger's distant vision derives first of all from the face of this land; from almost any mountain eminence—slope, saddle, pass, ridge, summit—one can see a long ways. The thin, high, dry comparatively dustless atmosphere magnifies these vistas as does the absence of human settlement. In the Rockies, only other mountains interfere with the view. This country is vast, it is enormous; it creates a perception of space even greater.

But I cannot help but wonder how old man Bridger might react today were he able to return and retrace his route from a spring hunt in the lower Wind Rivers toward one of the southerly rendezvous sites; Cache Valley in Utah, and Ham's Fork in southwestern Wyoming are both equally apt. The way down from South Pass bends beneath the Oregon Buttes and then a ragged volcanic plug known as Boar's Tusk before cutting into the Leucite Hills, and among those, in 1975, passing an enormous, new, coal-fired power plant: a triumph of cement and steel bulking out of nowhere in these high, earthen swells. On first spotting this, Bridger would no doubt have to rein in his horses and stare. But having encountered several lifetimes of strange sights already, he'd probably press on cautiously for a closer look. Whereupon he'd discover that this throbbing behemoth bears his own name—"The Jim Bridger Project: An Industrial Trailblazer—1,500,000 Kilowatts of Electric Energy."

For all I know, the old boy's eyes would water with pride; history has never really given him his due. More likely, he'd be utterly confused, possibly a little standoffish as well. All speculation of course, and in the end I can only think that the name Bridger has been vilified. Call a Wilderness Area after him, and a National Forest, a mountain pass, a high lake, a clear creek, as has justly been done, but perhaps not an air-cluttering power plant and the strip mine which feeds it.

Is this mere irony, or is it parable? No meaner question haunts the Rockies today.

By the turn of the century, the halcyon days of gold and silver were past and the Rocky Mountains settled into more than 50 years of quiet, slow growth based mainly on agriculture. As early as the 1870s, savvy ranchers realized that the sprawling basins of the region grew "gold from the grass roots up" in the form of free graze for as many beef cattle as could be punched over the land. By the turn of the century, cowpokes and sheepmen had pushed their stock high into the mountains as well to take advantage of the lush summer meadows. Farming progressed more slowly, needing a boost both from irrigation and a man's willingness to risk crop ruin from unseasonal frosts.

Perhaps the modern era of the Rockies began back in 1889 when Pennsylvania oilman Phillip Martin Shannon began filing claims in central Wyoming's Salt Creek Field, the first impulse in a rolling sequence that now sees the region *en route* to becoming the rest of the nation's energy colony. Or perhaps that historic moment is more recent, say in 1936 when a group of Hollywood film luminaries supplied the lustre necessary to launch the Rockies' first ski-based land boom at Sun Valley, Idaho: signal to the rest of the nation that here was a recreational playground it had overlooked.

Whatever its origins, a new episode in the Rockies was emergent in the 1950s, accelerating in the 1960s, veering in precarious control in the 1970s. This is no isolated process. The accidental conjunction of geology, climate and the westward dash of American history has left this region as the last great enclave of attractive open space in the contiguous 48 states. The stongest energies of national expansion skirted the mountains as they pushed on to Oregon and California; they swung south into Texas; they opted for industrial growth in the Northeast, the upper Midwest. While the more choice and productive environments elsewhere in the U. S. filled with people who worked them over, the less hospitable mountains remained a national leftover: largely open, a haven for the hardy few, a reclusive region—an old-fashioned place of doggedness, determination and grit.

The modern Rockies are less like this every day; vast expanses of open space, be they defined in terms of a region or a state, have always held a special lure to this peculiarly restless, yearning nation known as America. It's the old fable of the promised land and its fulfillment takes on many forms: a fresh start, a new life, 800 billion tons of coal, a two-acre lot for a second home, deep powder snow, enough molybdenum to last the nation 80 years, peace, quiet, the mountains, the view, whatever.

Save for scattered mining and areas of heavy overgrazing by sheep, the Rocky Mountain high country today remains largely untouched. But as one descends to the lower, less severe subalpine climes, the face of this land grows more marred. The broad gauntlet of supporting, middle elevation ecosystems—the dense stands of spruce and fir, the lush aspen groves, the valleys of meadowland and oakbrush and sage which are the lifelines of the regional watershed—all are changing. And often change means being replaced. A valley sinks beneath a slackwater lake fronted by a dam, or gives way to a skein of high-rise resorts or a crosshatch subdivision. A rolling woodland is penetrated by networks of roads leading to patches logged clean of every tree. Sod is turned "wrong side up," and in a dry spell begins to blow away. A mountaintop is removed to make way for an open pit copper mine. Winter storms are seeded to increase "water production," but the deeper snowpack buries forage vital to the survival of bighorn sheep, deer, elk. Taco stands, trailer courts, transmission lines and neon appear in pastures as if by spontaneous generation.

Living in the Rockies it is easy to be of two minds about this multiple carving of the land. Each new time I travel west from Denver I am struck by the vast wilds around me; from a Frontier Airlines 737 winging north or west or south, the impression magnifies, becomes even more reassuring. "Nothing," I absently think to myself, "can undo all this. This land is too immense, too far beyond our powers to sully. Surely there will be some that is left alone." In the Rockies it is easy to succumb to the illusion of plenty, but on those same journeys out of Denver, I can also see growing signs of the final invasion. Years ago Bernard DeVoto called the West "a plundered province"; the phrase has worn all too well. Today that plunder increases—a little bit here, a bit more there—an inexorable attrition: uneasy symptom of an affluent, consuming nation on its terminal glut.

As for the prospect: the technology to pump streams backward (uphill through holes bored in mountains) has been demonstrated; a plan for interring entire canyons beneath sooty mine waste has been aired and its execution seems only a matter of time. If we wish, we can convert forests to lumber plantations, harness Yellowstone's geysers for geothermal energy, or grow bananas on Pikes Peak.

The plunder is destined to press on. That psychological breaking point we must reach before we feel the urge to stop, is well down the road. For now, that infinitesimal envelope of time known as American history hastens toward its greatest conclusion which will also be its greatest shock. Open space, with its perennial gift of the opportunity to go West ("young man, go West"), move on, hit the trail, always to something better, has for over 350 years been an alluring emptiness into which this nation has grown. It is now the cornerstone of some of our most deeply embedded national assumptions. Open space has shaped our sense of promise; it has formed our very capacity to hope, to envision possibilities and to imagine what that wonderful word "future" might mean.

For this reason alone these mountains are well worth watching over. The Rockies are no longer leftovers; south of that giant landscape Alaska, they are the last vast reach of open space remaining in America. We need our tomorrows, even though they only be metaphors.

EPILOGUE: RETURN TO THE RIDGE

In the end, though, the mountains force me to seek an even grander perspective, perhaps as a refuge, perhaps as an explanation of the Rockies' peculiar spell which seems far greater than the civilization to which they now belong. In my mind I return to my nameless, 13,150-foot ridge in the Sangre de Cristo. This time as I wander by the lakes, I have no doubts about where on the fishhook I should climb, no fears that I'll not make it to the top. Once again it's a steep scramble, but now when I reach the summit no tide of clouds beats against the range and billows round Kit Carson Peak.

Instead the sky is bright, brittle and blue; the air clear, the mountains outlined like ice. All stands hard and still, but most of all the overwhelming presence of rock. The slabbed gray face of a peak, a jutting outcrop, a fractured boulder, a small angular chunk. Not a thing seems changed since I was last here. This rock—its firmness, its mass, its still shapes and the barriers it poses—all appear frozen, somehow beyond death and extinction.

I hunch out of my pack and sit wearily, buoyantly on the tundra: begin to relax, sink in. Nothing like rock to make one feel comfortable, to convey that soothing illusion of timelessness. Our strange yearning for something that will last.

Folly, of course, for in the end even rock is a child of time. No matter that it seems so solid, that it has existed for millions of years. As I sit atop my ridge, I know it is being levelled, bit by grain, toward the ultimate featureless plain which is the fate of all mountains. Know that it can do nothing else. Know this will happen in slow time, just as I will more swiftly grow old, will no longer climb this glorious ridge, and will die.

The squeak of a pika breaks my reverie, then a flutter of wind. Suddenly I am quickened and alert. Time to get established—find a flat spot, clear away the rocks, pitch tent, organize my little space in the wilderness. A little lightheaded, I set about my business—a troglodyte plodding the tundra under his pack.

Perched on a broken slab two miles and more above the sea, the pika quavers in noisy protest, then falls silent, for this is his home. Motionless and intent, he watches me as I methodically make camp.

The Red River in winter's deep freeze, Red River Basin, northern New Mexico. Left: Indian paintbrush glow like burning coals in the legendary Sangre de Cristo Range, New Mexico.

Remembrances of a gold-and-silver past. Lone Horse Mill on the Crystal River, Elk Range, Colorado. Right: Bridal Veil Falls and an old time mill above Telluride, San Juan Range.

Rincon of the Sangre de Cristo Range forms natural trap for wind carrying sand off the broad San Luis Valley, Great Sand Dunes National Monument. Right: Snow drifts below the Sierra Blanca (Blanca Peak 14,338 feet), Colorado.

August cumulus wash up on flanks of Kit Carson Peak (14,165 feet) Sangre de Cristo. Left: Ceaseless winds form sand waves below Sierra Blanca Peaks, Sangre de Cristo Range, Great Sand Dunes National Monument, Colorado.

Crestone Needle (14,191 feet), Sangre de Cristo Range, Colorado.
Right: Lake Fork Peak, Wheeler Peak Wilderness, New Mexico.

Winter's ice angel, Colorado River in Glenwood Canyon, western Colorado. Right: Autumn snow highlights the terraced flanks of South and North Maroon Peaks, Maroon Bells-Snowmass Wilderness, Elk Range, Colorado. Pages 56-57: The red strata of the Maroon formation counterpoint the somber granitic grays of Snowmass Mountain high in the Elk Range near Aspen, Colorado.

Spring freeze captures flying water droplets along upper Roaring Fork river, Sawatch Range. Right: Natural spray of Columbine below Maroon Bells, Elk Range, Colorado.

A winter sunrise strikes the old mining town of Leadville, two miles high in central Colorado. In the distance 14,421 foot Mount Massive. Right: Autumn casts its delicate orange touch upon the canyons above Snowmass in Colorado's Elk Range.

A lone glacial erratic in North Park below Mount Zirkel (12,810 feet) and the Park Range near Walden, Colorado. Left: The Diamond, a sheer 2,000 foot wall on the east face of Longs Peak (14,256 feet), catches the sun's first rays above Chasm Lake, Front Range, Rocky Mountain National Park, Colorado.

Pikes Peak (14,110 feet) mythic, massive and magnificent, looms high above the tilted sandstone fins of the Garden of the Gods, Front Range. Right: Spring snows freeze and thaw on a ledge before Mt. Champion, Sawatch Range, Colorado.

Buckwheat and Indian paintbrush in aspen grove, Rabbit
Ears Range. Left: July along Maroon Canyon, Elk Range, Colorado.

Pages 68-69: Autumn's flaming finale below Pyramid Peak (14,018 feet) and Maroon Bells in the Elk Range. Left: Rydbergia, the dwarfed alpine sunflower, dance on the tundra, Rocky Mountain National Park. Above: Eroded Precambrian rock on Trail Ridge frames Longs Peak (14,256 feet), Colorado.

Mountain goats ease over high ledges of the Sawatch Range.
Left: Prominent ridges of Mount Evans (14,264 feet) and Mount Bierstadt above the Abyss Lake basin. The serrated Gore Range marks the distant western horizon, Colorado.

Fleeting summer storm trails a veil of fog on the ridges of Mount Bierstadt (14,060 feet). Right: A delicate spray of phlox mingles with crustose lichen on granite; this typifies the alpine world atop Mount Evans, Front Range, Colorado.

A lone angler wades the July flow of Bear River, Flattops Wilderness, Colorado. Left: Roaring Fork Creek tumbles below the east face of Longs Peak, Rocky Mountain National Park.

The meandering headwaters of the Arkansas River and Mount Elbert (14,433 feet), the Rockies' highest, Sawatch Range. Right: The inevitable aftermath of running water and slow time, Black Canyon of the Gunnison National Monument, Colorado; the river has carved a 2000 foot gorge in the darkened rock.

Graceful bloom of the shooting star in Snowy Range, Wyoming.
Left: Lake Marie reflects the rocky facade of Medicine Bow Peak (12,013 feet) in the Snowy Range.

Upper Red Castle Lake and Red Castle Peak, Uinta Mountains, Utah.
Left: Mount Superior, above Alta, Wasatch Range, Utah, Pages 84-85:
Freeze-fractured monolith on the Beartooth Plateau, Montana.

Alpine avens in a tundra wilderness, Beartooth Plateau above the Rock Creek drainage, Montana. Left: Lupine bloom in alpine meadows, Beartooth Plateau. Pages 88-89: Granite Glacier clings tenaciously to north face of Granite Peak (12,799 feet), Montana's high point, Beartooth Mountains.

A circle of glacial debris holds a small tarn in the vast tundra country on Hellroaring Plateau, Beartooth Mountains, Montana. Left: Above the boiling summer clouds on Hellroaring Plateau.

Glacier fed lakes 2000 feet below the summit of Cloud Peak (13,167 feet), Big Horn Range, Wyoming. Left: Alpine avens cluster between the granites on Horse Ridge, Wind River Range, Wyoming.

The singular block of Squaretop Mountain mirrored in the becalmed Green River Lakes; historic trapping country of the Wind River Range, Wyoming. Left: Summer cumulus float above Fremont and Jackson Peaks in the Wind River Range.

Wilderness face of a Rocky Mountain Bighorn Sheep. Right: A jagged serac on the Continental Divide from the summit of Fremont Peak includes Mounts Sacajawea (13,502 feet), Helen (13,620 feet), Warren (13,720 feet) and Woodrow Wilson (13,502 feet); in the distance is Gannet Peak (13,785 feet), Wyoming's highest, Wind River Range. Page 98: Glacial erratics strewn on the bedrock of Titcomb Basin below Woodrow Wilson Peak and The Sphinx. Page 99: Cirque of Towers from Mitchell Peak with Pingora and Wolfs Head, Wind River Range, Wyoming.

A still moment on Deep Lake reflects the solitary world of Temple (13,249 feet) and East Temple (12,976 feet) Peaks. Bridger Wilderness in the Wind River Range, Wyoming.

Breeze-strewn ripples create a hypnotic design on Lonesome Lake, Popo Agie Wilderness, Wind River Range, Wyoming. Left: Morning sun on Warrior Ridge above Lonesome Lake, Cirque of Towers. Pages 104-105: Evening quiet, Echo Lake and Gannett Peak, Glacier Wilderness, Wind River Range.

The icy facade of Dinwoody Glaciers seen from Horse Ridge.
Left: The flush of an August sunrise on Gannett Peak above
Echo Lake in Glacier Wilderness, Wind River Range, Wyoming.

Mistake Lake reflections, Bridger Wilderness, Wind River Range, Wyoming. Right: The glacier-carved west face of Fremont Peak with Twin Peaks across Titcomb Basin, Bridger Wilderness.

Profuse bloom of the Elephant head and Indian paintbrush along Seneca Lake, Bridger Wilderness, Wyoming. Left: Lone campsite on rocky shores of Island Lake in the Wind River Range.

Pink monkey flowers are commonly seen along creeksides in the late summer. Left: A mountain creek splashes down a stony staircase in the Bridger Wilderness, Wyoming.

The fiery orb of an October sunrise, Grand Teton from Pierre's Hole, once the site of a fur trappers' rendezvous in eastern Idaho. Right: Moonrise over the Grand Teton (13,776 feet) and Mount Owen, east of Driggs, Idaho.

A January sunrise bathes the Grand Teton in a momentary but timeless glow, Jackson Hole, northwestern Wyoming.

A happy crew of river rats pilot the wild Snake River below Jackson, Wyoming. Right: The Teton Range under a passing canopy of clouds at sunrise. Pages 120-121: The evening summer sun above the waters of Jenny Lake in the Grand Teton National Park, Wyoming.

The Grand Teton and Mount Owen appear above a cluster of Columbine in Cascade Canyon, Teton Range. Left: Trail Creek flow, Targhee National Forest, Wyoming.

Mists from a spring storm shroud the Tetons; Wyethia blooms brighten the somber sage flats of Jackson Hole, Wyoming. Left: Lichen's intricate design textures a granite boulder in Alaska Basin high in the Teton Range.

Winter feeding time in Jackson Hole. Right: Winter's symphony of peaks, water flowing and a mantle of white, Jackson Hole, Grand Teton National Park, Wyoming.

A lone bull elk forages in a driving mid-winter blizzard.
Right: The Upper Geyser Basin's premier attraction, Old Faithful, blows off steam, Yellowstone National Park.

Full antlered mule deer bucks forage on their winter range below the Bridger Wilderness. Right: The delicate pools of Minerva Terrace, Mammoth Hot Springs, Yellowstone National Park. Pages 132-133: Borah Peak (12,662 feet), Idaho's highest, dominates the Lost River Range.

Alpine phlox and saxifrage. Right: Sunrise on the Chinese Wall (11,238 feet), White Cloud Peaks, Idaho. Pages 136-137: Sawtooth Lake and Wilderness, Idaho.

Moss gentian in fellfield. Left: Lofty granites frame Mt. Cramer (10,716 feet) above Redfish Basin, Sawtooth Range.

The reflective solitude of a May sunrise, Stanley Lake, Sawtooth Range. Left: Summer advances on iced-in Alpine Lake in the Sawtooth Wilderness, Idaho.

Mount Heyburn dominates the granite ridge above Stanley, Idaho. Right: A chill October morning along Kane Creek, The Devil's Bedstead (11,051 feet), Pioneer Range, Idaho.

Weather-sculptured roots of whitebark pine at timberline.
Left: Little Boulder Creek and Castle Peak (11,815 feet) deep among the tumbled mazes of the White Cloud Range, Idaho.

The Salmon River near Challis, Idaho. Left: Farm along East Fork, Salmon River. Pages 148-149: The great Divide and Lower St. Mary Lake, Glacier National Park, Montana.

Above right: Cherry blossoms beneath the Mission Range near Saint Ignatius, Montana. Above left: The Como Peaks (9,624 feet) and apple blossoms in the Bitterroot Valley near Hamilton. Left: Mission Mountains near Ronan.

A weathered barn and the snowclad Mission Range. Right:
The distant ridges of the Continental Divide broods
above a sea of waving wheat near Augusta, Montana.

Reynolds Mountain (9,147 feet) towers above an assemblage of flowering beargrass, Glacier National Park, Montana. Left: A mosaic of water-worn cobbles in McDonald Creek.

Midsummer floes in Iceberg Lake, Glacier National Park, Montana.
Left: Icy interior of Sperry Glacier, once the largest in the Park, now half the size as when first explored in 1897.

On top of the Continent. Bearhat Mountain (8,740 feet)
and Hidden Lake. Right: Hidden Lake nestles in classic cirque
from Reynolds Mountain, Glacier National Park.

Summer splash of wild flowers in Hanging Gardens below the Garden Wall. Left: Crevasse and boulder tumble headlong downward in Sexton Glacier ice fall, Glacier National Park, Montana.

Heavily muscled Big Horn rams on their spring range above Many Glacier. Left: Snow laced Reynolds Mountain nudges clouds along the Continental Divide. Pages 164-165: A rank of glacier-hewn peaks holds a spring storm around St. Mary Lake, Glacier National Park, Montana.

Cobbles along St. Mary Lake, Glacier Park. Right: Western larch and Mt. Warren, Anaconda-Pintlar Wilderness, Montana.

Summer moonset on Como Peaks of the Bitterroot Range.
Left: Timber Creek Falls in the Crazy Mountains, Montana.

Woodland pattern of bunchberry dogwood along the Middle Fork, Flathead River, Montana. Right: A fern crown and Western red cedar, Avalanche Creek, Glacier National Park.

A tree squirrel makes short order of a lodgepole cone.
Left: Sub-alpine fir and cones above Moon Lake in the Mission Range, western Montana.

Bearded steeplejack of the Rockies, a mountain goat high above Gunsight Pass, Glacier National Park. Right: Bird's eye view from the Garden Wall of McDonald Creek Valley and the Livingston Range during summer rains.

St. Nicholas Mountain (9,380 feet) looms over the bony ridges near Dawson Pass, Glacier National Park. Left: Pest and delight, the raucous Clark's Nutcracker in flight.

Mountain goat above Lake Ellen Wilson, Glacier National Park, Montana. Right: A primal staircase of glacial tiers, lakes and spires along the great Divide. Flinsch Peak (9,225 feet) and Mt. Stimson (10,155 feet) from the flank of Rising Wolf Mountain.

Starburst reflection, Swiftcurrent Lake, Glacier National Park, Montana.

Wild Goose Island in St. Mary Lake below Gunsight and Fusillade Mountains, Glacier National Park, Montana. Left: Ice pattern and ground-hugging mat of pink moss campion.

Sinopah Mountain rises high above Two Medicine Lake, Glacier National Park, Montana. Right: Quaking aspen and St. Mary Lake, September.

Afternoon sun cascades over the Teton Range, Jackson Hole, Wyoming. Right: Torrents of spring, snowmelt freshets plummet from the Hanging Garden, Glacier National Park, Montana.

ABOUT THIS BOOK

The Rockies are an immense province of scattered mountain ridges and valleys . . . from my first exhilarating sight, a great love evolved for exploring their alpine heights. Early dreams of trekking in and visually experiencing the whole range—from the Sangre de Cristos to Glacier—have flourished. This portfolio is a focus on an unending journey—an affair revealing my experience—in the Rockies. From the beginning it was a vision to thread a near impossible theme of simplicity—to avoid effects of fragmentation and relate intuitively impressions of the whole range, yet impart some minute details—that are so much an expression of the Universal experience. I hope this encounter with beauty—rhythms of mountains and water—will manifest an awareness for our American heritage and preserve it the way Nature created it.

The photographs in this portfolio were made with both a 4x5 Linhof Teknika, using daylight ektachrome film and a 35mm Leicaflex SLR, using kodachrome 11 film. Exposures calculated from a Weston lightmeter. Lenses were 75mm through 500mm for the 4x5 and 21mm through 560mm for 35mm work. A few filters were used sparingly to fill a gap between what I saw and what the film actually records. A tripod was essential in most instances with exception for the elusive animal images, and precarious, windy, high rock situations where a sturdy setting was impossible. Elevations given for mountains in many instances vary considerably. THE FOURTEENERS, by Perry Eberhart and Philip Schmuck; WIND RIVER RANGE FIELD BOOK, by Orrin and Lorraine Bonney; GUIDE TO THE COLORADO MOUNTAINS, by Robert Ormes; and USGS Topographic maps provided assistance in elevations given in captions. A special thanks to David Sumner for his contribution of photographs on pages 51 and 176.

ACKNOWLEDGEMENTS

My thanks to the following good people for their help in making the text of this book possible. To Dr. Don Baars of Fort Lewis College, Durango, Colorado; Dr. J. D. Ives of the Institute of Arctic and Alpine Research, Boulder, Colorado and Dr. Estella Leopold of the U.S. Geological Survey, Denver for their scrutiny of my errant facts. To George Kelly of Cortez, Colorado and Whit Porter of Denver for badly needed editorial counsel. To Merrill G. Hastings, publisher of Colorado Magazine for showing me some things about feeling and caring for the mountains. To Ernie Wilkinson, Rob Nickens, Ray Stebbins and Judy Sumner for exploring the high country with me. And to a couple of dogs named Gus and Ralf for invaluable companionship on my otherwise solitary journeys into the Rockies.